take **5** geography

Seas & Oceans

Jane & Steve Parker

Consultant: Keith Lye

W

FRANKLIN WATTS

A Division of Grolier Publishing

NEW YORK • LONDON • HONG KONG • SYDNEY
DANBURY, CONNECTICUT

First American Edition 1998 by
Franklin Watts
A Division of Grolier Publishing Co., Inc.
90 Sherman Turnpike
Danbury, Connecticut 06816

Library of Congress Cataloging-in-Publication Data

Parker, Jane, 1951–
    Seas and oceans / Jane & Steve Parker : consultant, Keith Lye.
        p.   cm. — (Take 5 geography)
    Includes index.
    Summary: An overview of the rich and varied environments of the earth's
seas and oceans, as exemplified by five of the most famous of them.
    ISBN 0–531–14459–3
    1. Ocean—Juvenile literature.   [1. Ocean.]   I. Parker, Steve.
II. Title.   III. Series.
GC21.5.P36 1998
551.46—dc21

                         97–29104
                            CIP
                                AC

Series editor: Kyla Barber
Designer: Ness Wood
Illustrator: Joanna Biggs
Picture researcher: Susan Mennell
Art director: Robert Walster
Consultant: Keith Lye

Printed in Great Britain

Photographic credits:

t=top, b=bottom, c=center, l=left, r=right
Cover photo, Robert Harding, Douglas Peebles;
4, Robert Harding;
5, Planet Earth Pictures, Peter Scoones;
7 t, Planet Earth Pictures, Verena Tunnicliffe;
7 b, Planet Earth Pictures, Robert Hessler;
8, Robert Harding, Liaison Int.;
9, Bruce Coleman, G Ziesler;
10 t, The Hutchison Library, Bernard Régent;
10 b, Robert Harding;
11 l, Images;
11 r, Images;
12, Images;
13 l, Planet Earth Pictures, Paolo Fanciulli;
13 r, Planet Earth Pictures, Flip Schulke/NASA;
14 t, NHPA, A.N.T.;
14 b, Planet Earth Pictures, Gary Bell;
15 l, FLPA, D P Wilson;
15 r, Bruce Coleman, Orion Service & Trading Co Inc;
16 t, Bruce Coleman, Jeff Foott Productions;
16 b, FLPA, E & D Hosking;
17 t, Images;
17 b, Images;
18, Bruce Coleman, Guido Cozzi;
19 t, AKG, Erich Lessing *Neptune's Steed* by Walter Crane, 1992, Munich, Bayer. Staatsgemaeldesammlungen;
19 r, Mary Evans;
20 t, Colorific!, Mirella Ricciardi;
20 b, © National Maritime Museum Picture Library, *Death of Vitus Bering* by Christian Julins Lodewy Portman (neg. no. BHCO359)
21 l, Seaco Picture Library;
21 r, Bridgeman Art Library *Viking Ship* by H Oakes-Jones (Private Collections);
22 t, Planet Earth Pictures, Hans Christian Heap;
22 b, Still Pictures, Michel Gunther;
23 l, Planet Earth Pictures, Ian Ball;
23 r, Colorific!, Bryan & Cherry Alexander;
24, Telegraph Colour Library;
25 t, NHPA, A.N.T.;
25 bl, Images;
25 br, Bruce Coleman, Neville Coleman;
26 t, Seaco Picture Library;
26 b, Images;
27 l, Planet Earth Pictures, Dick Clarke;
27 r, Christine Osborne;
28 bl, NHPA, David Woodfall;
28 tr, Colorific!, J Kettmar/Allstock;
29 t, Bruce Coleman, Worldwide Fund for Nature;
29 b, FLPA, E & D Hosking;
31, Images.

Contents

What Are Seas and Oceans?

It's been five days since the ship sank. On the life raft, under the blazing sun, you are hungry and thirsty. The clear sky and the endless water, with its gently lapping waves, dazzle your eyes with their blueness. Occasionally a seabird flies overhead. A fin appears above the surface! Friendly dolphin or lurking shark? At any moment, a storm could blow up. You are all alone, in the middle of the ocean.

Sea or ocean?

We call our planet "Earth." But a better name might be "Water," or even "Salt Water." More than seven-tenths of the earth's surface are covered by the salty water of seas and oceans.

Oceans are the largest bodies of salt water. The four main ones are the Pacific, Atlantic, Indian, and Arctic. Sometimes the waters around Antarctica are described as the Southern Ocean. Seas are smaller than oceans and are usually around coastlines or islands. There are about fifty main named seas, including the Mediterranean, Caribbean, and Bering seas.

Bigger than all the rest

The largest ocean is the Pacific. It covers more than a third of the earth's surface and is almost as big as the other three oceans together. It's the deepest too, averaging 14,100 feet (4,300m) in depth.

The seas and oceans of the world are home to a huge variety of animals. This sea turtle comes ashore only to lay eggs.

Areas in millions of square miles (sq km): **Pacific Ocean:** 69 (180); **Atlantic Ocean:** 37 (94);

FIVE WORLD SEAS & OCEANS

ARCTIC OCEAN

GREENLAND

RUSSIA

CANADA

BERING

CHINA

USA

ATLANTIC

EUROPE

MEDITERRANEAN

INDIA

PACIFIC

CARIBBEAN

AFRICA

N

BRAZIL

AUSTRALIA

W E

S

ANTARCTICA

Take 5 seas and oceans

Pacific Ocean is studded with about 25,000 islands, more than all other seas and oceans together. It is home to Polynesian and Melanesian peoples with unique cultures.

Atlantic Ocean was once teeming with fish, seals, and whales—but has our mass slaughter endangered their survival?

Mediterranean Sea had some of the world's oldest civilizations around its shores, including the Egyptians, Minoans, Greeks, Phoenicians, and Romans.

Caribbean Sea is a tourist tropical holiday paradise. But pollution and poverty in some areas threaten the existence of wildlife and beautiful coral reefs.

Bering Sea is far in the north. It is cold, choppy, windy, foggy, and ice-covered in winter. Yet fur seals and other creatures thrive in its undisturbed waters.

So Salty, You Float!

The "salt" in seawater is halite (sodium chloride)—the same substance as cooking or table salt. Normal seawater is about one-thirtieth dissolved salt, plus smaller amounts of other minerals. But the Dead Sea, landlocked between Jordan and Israel, is almost one-third dissolved salt! Hardly any living thing can survive in it, which is how the sea got its name. The dissolved salt makes the water so thick and heavy, or dense, that people float like corks. In the area's hot climate, the Dead Sea is slowly drying out and becoming even more salty!

You cannot sink in the Dead Sea—its water is too dense!

Mediterranean Sea: 1.1 (3); **Caribbean Sea:** 0.96 (2.5); **Bering Sea:** 0.89 (2.3).

Lands Under the Water

The floors of the seas and oceans are mostly hidden from us in the depths. But we know that there are towering mountains, sheer cliffs, winding valleys, plunging canyons, and vast flat plains. How? From echo sounding, or sonar scans. Pictures of the ocean floor are formed by sending down sound waves from the surface and detecting the echoes.

The continental shelf

Around each main landmass, or continent, is a ledgelike area of the "continental shelf." It is only about 650 to 980 feet (200 to 300m) below the surface of the land, so the sea is shallow. The sun filters through the water making it light and warm, so plants and animals thrive. At the shelf edge the "continental slope" drops to the depths.

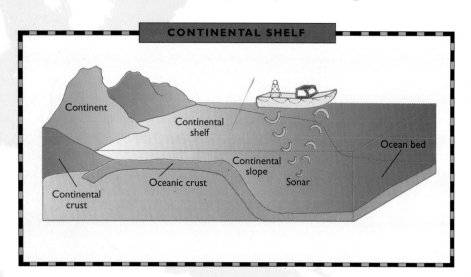

CONTINENTAL SHELF

Continent

Continental shelf

Ocean bed

Continental slope

Sonar

Oceanic crust

Continental crust

The seabed, or ocean floor, becomes deeper in stages, from the continental shelf to the continental slope and finally the deep sea. The depth of the ocean floor can be measured by sending down sonar signals from a boat and recording the echoes.

Abyssal plains

These massive flat areas, covered with mud, stretch away from the continental slope, out into midocean. The water is mostly between 6,500 and 13,000 feet (2,000 and 4,000m) deep. At the bottom it is pitch black and very cold. The world's strangest-looking creatures live here.

Average depths in feet: **Pacific:** 14,110; **Atlantic:** 12,140; **Bering:** 5,250;

Oceanic ridges

The earth's outer layers are divided into huge, jigsawlike pieces called lithospheric plates. These drift slowly around, carrying the land with them. In some places, beneath the sea, these plates are moving apart. Incredibly hot, runny rock from deep within the earth wells up at a crack between the two plates. It cools and becomes solid, adding to the plates' edges and making them larger. A double row of mountains, called an "oceanic ridge," forms at the crack. This process, "seafloor spreading," widens the Atlantic by 2 inches (5cm) each year.

Ocean floors are created at oceanic ridges and destroyed at deep-sea trenches.

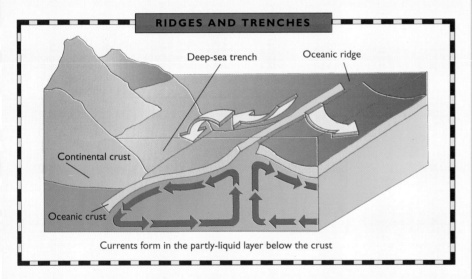

RIDGES AND TRENCHES

Deep-sea trench

Oceanic ridge

Continental crust

Oceanic crust

Currents form in the partly-liquid layer below the crust

Deep-sea trenches

In other places, plates collide. One plate edge may be pushed below the edge of its neighbor. This process, "subduction," forms a deep-sea trench. The biggest is the Marianas Trench, in the northwest Pacific at 1,550 miles (2,500km) long. One part of it plunges to a depth of 35,799 feet (10,911m) below sea level. It is the lowest point on the earth's surface. A large stone would take more than one hour to sink to the bottom.

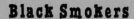

Chemicals and gases from deep within the earth bubble up out of black smoking vents.

On the deep seabed there are cracks where incredibly hot water and dark clouds of chemicals bubble up from deep within the earth. Around these hydrothermal vents, or "black smokers," live arm-sized worms, pale blind crabs, and other unusual creatures.

Giant tube worms live near vents.

Moving Waters

The waters of seas and oceans are never still. Great flowing currents, called gyres, swirl around the oceans. Smaller currents move waters around seas and bays. Waves crash onto the shoreline. And the tide rises and falls in a never-ending, unbroken pattern.

The waters of our seas and oceans are pushed and pulled by the forces of both tides and currents.

Ocean currents

Large-scale movements of water are driven mainly by winds. As the earth rotates, currents form huge circular movements which circle clockwise in the oceans of the Northern Hemisphere (everywhere north of the equator) and counterclockwise in the Southern Hemisphere (south of the equator). The shapes of landmasses also affect the directions of currents. These currents occur mainly in the top 1,150 feet (350m) of the oceans, but there are other, deeper currents. Cold, "heavy" polar water flows toward the equator, replacing warm, "light" surface water that flows toward the poles.

Major ocean currents move seawater around the world. The blue arrows show cool currents, the red show warm.

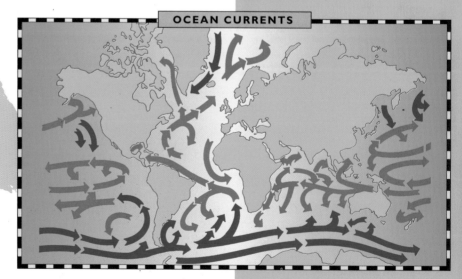

OCEAN CURRENTS

Important ocean currents: **Pacific:** El Nino ("The Child"); **Atlantic:** Gulf Stream;

Vertical currents

Ocean currents can also move up and down, circulating water from the depths to the surface, and back again. This is due to variations in the temperature of seawater in different parts of the world. It is also caused by variations in the water's saltiness. The saltier the water, the heavier (denser) it is, so it sinks. As it mixes with the surrounding water it becomes less salty and rises back to the surface again.

Time and tide

Tides are caused mainly by the moon. Its gravity, or pulling force, tugs a "bulge" of ocean water toward it. As the moon goes around the earth, this bulge is dragged around with it. On the earth's surface, we see the passing of the bulge as the rise and fall of the tide, once every 12 hours 25 minutes.

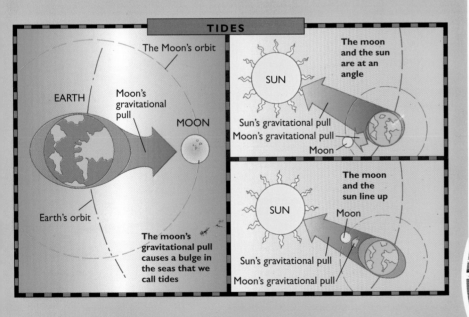

TIDES

The Moon's orbit

EARTH

Moon's gravitational pull

MOON

Earth's orbit

The moon's gravitational pull causes a bulge in the seas that we call tides

The moon and the sun are at an angle

SUN

Sun's gravitational pull
Moon's gravitational pull
Moon

The moon and the sun line up

SUN

Moon

Sun's gravitational pull
Moon's gravitational pull

The difference between high and low tides varies. When the moon and sun line up, as shown above, their pulling forces add together to cause spring tides, which are extra high and extra low. If the moon and sun don't align, their forces partly cancel out, causing tides with much less range.

Around Antarctica

Very cold water flows around the great southern continent of Antarctica, in a clockwise, or westerly, direction, through what is sometimes called the Southern Ocean. This is the Antarctic Circumpolar Current. It is driven by cool westerly winds coming down from South America, Africa, and Australasia, and counter-clockwise ocean currents circulating in the South Pacific, South Atlantic, and Indian oceans. The Antarctic Circumpolar Current moves an incredible 185 million tons of water every second.

Antarctica's ocean currents sweep icebergs and ice sheets from its shores.

Mediterranean: Gibraltar Current; **Caribbean:** North Equatorial Current; **Bering:** Aleutian Current.

Water Versus Land

Land and sea wage an endless battle. In some places land wins. It grows outward into the sea, building shingle spits, sandbars, mudflats, and salt marshes. In other places the sea wins. Its waves wash away beaches and eat into cliffs. As a result, coastlines are slowly but constantly changing.

Eventually, these arches will collapse into rubble and be swept away.

The highest wave ever recorded was in a Pacific typhoon. It was estimated to be 111 feet (34m) from base to crest.

Wind and waves

Far out in the deep midocean, steady winds pile the water into huge ripples, called swell. In the Atlantic, the swell can be more than 82 feet (25m) high. Boats rise on one ridge, or peak, then seem to disappear as they descend into the trough before the next peak.

As these great ripples approach shallow water, their ridges pile higher and higher, as ocean rollers. Finally they crash onto the shore as breakers. The stronger the wind, and the greater the distance it blows across the ocean or sea, the bigger the waves.

Winds whip swell into "white horses."

Temperature ranges of surface water: **Pacific:** 32°F to 86°F; **Atlantic:** 36°F to 84°F;

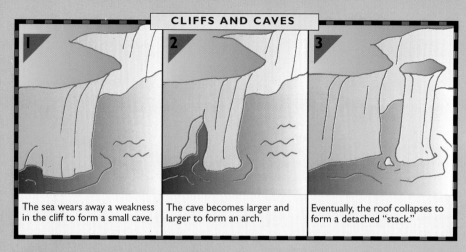

CLIFFS AND CAVES

1. The sea wears away a weakness in the cliff to form a small cave.

2. The cave becomes larger and larger to form an arch.

3. Eventually, the roof collapses to form a detached "stack."

Cliffs and caves

Around the coasts, waves pick up pebbles and sand grains and hurl them at beaches and cliffs. The cliff base is gouged into hollows and caves. The overhang above collapses to form a shelf called a "wave cut platform" littered with boulders. The continuing waves and currents gradually wear down the boulders into pebbles and sand grains.

Drifting shores

Winds usually blow waves at an angle against the shore. Along with inshore currents, they move rocks, pebbles, sand, and mud along the coast—a process called longshore drift. These forces can pile up shingle and sand as spits, bars, and flats, which grow into the sea or across a bay.

Chesil Beach, a shingle spit in Dorset, England, grows several feet a year.

Holding Back the Sea

The Netherlands is a low-lying country bordering the North Sea. Over one-third of its land has been reclaimed from the sea and is below high-tide level. The sea is kept out by building long, low walls, called dikes, around areas known as polders, and then pumping out the water. Windmills once did this job. Today the pumps are driven by diesel engines or electric motors. The former seabed provides rich, fertile soil for farming.

Windmills helped to keep the reclaimed land dry.

Mediterranean: 41°F to 88°F; **Caribbean:** 73°F to 84°F; **Bering:** 28°F to 50°F.

The Weather and the Sea

The Mediterranean climate, around the shores of the Mediterranean Sea, is a warm "maritime" climate. Because of the influence of the sea, it is generally neither too hot nor too cold. Summers are long, warm and dry—great for vacations—while winters are mild and moist. These conditions are ideal for growing crops like wheat, barley, grapes, olives, and oranges.

Many people enjoy the calm, sunny weather around the Mediterranean Sea.

Mild and moderate

Maritime climates are mild and pleasant because they are affected by the behavior of the sea itself. The weather over seas and oceans is not as extreme as the weather on land. This is because water neither absorbs nor loses the sun's heat as quickly as solid ground. So the sea does not become as cold in winter, nor as hot in summer, as the land.

Also, ocean currents continually spread the sun's heat around the globe. Coastal weather is also moderate, with milder winters and cooler summers than weather inland.

Weather conditions that affect waves in: **Pacific:** typhoons; **Atlantic:** doldrums;

Sea breezes and fogs

As the sun shines on the shore, the land heats up more quickly than the water. The air above it gets warm and rises, allowing cool air to blow in from the sea. This is an onshore breeze. At night, the land quickly becomes cooler than the sea, giving rise to the opposite effect, an offshore breeze.

Onshore winds bring moist air, containing invisible water vapor. As it cools over land, it forms tiny water droplets and makes sea mist and fog near the ground or clouds and rain higher up. Which is why the seaside is not always sunny!

A waterspout sucks up a great tube of water from the sea. If it moves over land it drops its load and may produce a shower of water and fish!

Tornado of water

In very hot, thundery conditions, pockets of warm air rise quickly and may create the swirling, funnel-shaped winds of a tornado. These generally occur over land, but when they happen at sea, they suck up seawater in a gigantic, spinning waterspout that skips across the ocean, lifting up fish, driftwood, and even boats.

Hurricane!

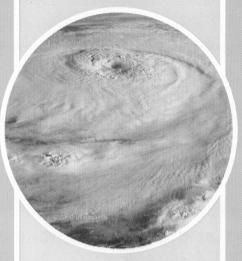

Swirling storm clouds speed up into hurricane-force winds.

Hurricanes are produced as warm air rises over a wide area forming great pillars of cloud. Cold air rushes in below and creates these spiraling storms. They are known as cyclones, or hurricanes, from a Carib word meaning "big wind." These storms form north of the equator out in the Atlantic Ocean. They cause terrible damage when they reach land. Similar storms in the Pacific are called typhoons, from the Chinese word for "great wind."

Mediterranean: Scirocco Winds; **Caribbean:** hurricanes; **Bering:** the Bering blizzards.

Life in Seas and Oceans

Life probably began in the seas, more than 3.5 billion years ago. The first living things were like microscopic blobs of jelly. The process of evolution, or change over time, has produced millions of different kinds of plants and animals, suited to every kind of marine (saltwater) habitat.

The great white shark, or white pointer, cruises warm seas and oceans all around the world.

Coral reefs

In warm seas like the Caribbean coral polyps flourish. These tiny animals catch tiny bits of floating food with their tentacles. They make hard, cup-shaped outer skeletons to protect and support their floppy bodies.

Over thousands of years, millions of corals grow, and their empty skeletons form the rocky caves and overhangs of the reef.

The branching coral growths shelter all kinds of sea creatures, such as lobsters, sea urchins, moray eels, and parrot fish.

Seas with coral reefs: **Pacific:** Hawaii; **Atlantic:** Bermuda; **Caribbean:** Turks and Caicos;

The rich shallows

In the Caribbean Sea, as in other seas and oceans, most plants and animals are found in the shallow waters near the shore. It is warmer, and enough sunlight can shine through the water, for seaweeds and other plants to grow. These marine plants are food and shelter for myriad creatures such as worms, limpets, mussels, crabs, shrimps, and small fish.

Open water

In the deeper open water, plants also grow. But they are not seaweeds. They are tiny floating algae, called phytoplankton. Small animals, zooplankton, feed on them. These include the young forms, or larvae, of many bigger fish and shellfish.

This planktonic "soup" is food for small fish, such as anchovies and herring, which are eaten by big predators like marlin and tuna.

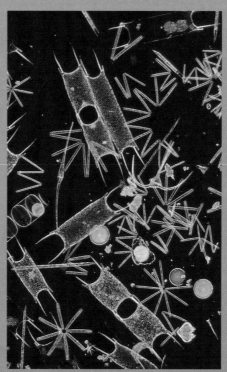

Many tiny species of plankton live in a single drop of seawater.

Life on the bottom

Even deep in the darkest, coldest depths of the Caribbean Sea, over 300 feet down, there is life. It is far too dark for plants to grow. But many kinds of worms, sea cucumbers, sea lilies, starfish, and crabs feed on the bits and pieces of dead animals and plants that sink down from nearer the surface.

Giants of the Depths

The Sea of Japan, between the islands of Japan and the Asian mainland, is not very large. But it is very deep. On the bottom live the world's biggest crabs—giant Japanese spider crabs. Their bodies are about the size of dinner plates and weigh up to 44 pounds (20kg). The spindly pincers and legs are enormously long, 13 feet (4m) from tip to tip! On the seabed, supported by water, the crab needs only tiny muscles to move its long limbs. But on land, without the support of water, it can hardly move at all.

A giant Japanese spider crab living in the deep waters of the Sea of Japan.

Mediterranean: no large reef areas; **Bering:** almost no coral at all—it's too cold for most species.

Journeys Through the Oceans

Some ocean creatures stay in the same bay or coral reef all their lives. But others wander the wide oceans. They may travel long distances each year to where conditions are better for feeding or breeding. These great journeys are called migrations.

Dolphins may leap to escape sharks or just for fun!

North for cool food

The Bering Sea is just south of the Arctic Circle, between Alaska on the west, the Kamchatka peninsula to the east, and the Pacific Ocean in the south. Being so far north, it is ice covered in the long, cold winter, and few creatures live there.

In summer, the sun shines strongly for a few months. Also, surface currents from the south bring warmer tropical waters northward. And vertical currents bring up rich nutrients from the depths. The tiny plants and animals of the plankton feed on these and thrive in their trillions. Shrimplike creatures called krill feed on the plankton in their billions, along with many small fish. The krill and fish, in turn, are eaten by terns and other seabirds, seals, and whales, who have flown and swum hundreds of miles from the south.

The Arctic tern migrates from the far north to the far south and back, each year. It covers 18,600 miles (30,000km) and never sees winter!

A blue whale eats 4.4 tons (4 tonnes) of its food, krill, every day!

Animals named after their regions: **Pacific:** salmon; **Atlantic:** manta ray;

Go south

In the autumn, the Bering Sea days become shorter and colder. Food grows scarce. So the seabirds, seals, and whales head south again, to warmer conditions in the Pacific, for winter. Great whales, like the humpback, blue, and gray, give birth to their calves in tropical shallows. The water is warm, but contains little food. So the whales live off the fat reserves stored in their bodies. When spring arrives they swim north again, on migrations of 3,100 miles (5,000km) or more, for the summer feast in the Bering Sea.

Humpback whales grow to more than 66 feet (20m) long.

Steller's sea lions breed on the shores around the Bering Sea.

Mediterranean: rock whelk; **Caribbean:** manatee; **Bering:** char (troutlike fish).

Spirits of the Seas

Seas and oceans influence people's lives in many ways, especially on small islands where the waters are all around! They affect the weather, provide a harvest of fish and shellfish, create a barrier against easy travel but also protection from attack, and form the basis of traditions, folklore, and tales of gods and spirits. Sailors and islanders are often very superstitious and have great respect for the powers and dangers of the ocean.

Island hopping

In ancient times, before the Greeks and Romans sailed the Mediterranean Sea, people from southern Asia were taking to simple boats, and stage by stage, they island hopped across the Pacific. As each group of islands was reached, some people stayed and settled.

No one knows who made the huge statues on Easter Island, in the Pacific.

They developed their own beliefs and customs, with gods and goddesses who protected them on their voyages and filled their nets with fish. Other people pushed onward to find new dots of land in the vast ocean.

Some experts believe that people also island hopped across the Pacific from the Americas. The *Kon Tiki* expedition of 1947 showed that currents could carry a raft of balsa (a light, strong wood) from Peru, where the Incas once lived, to Tahiti in the central Pacific.

Sea gods and myths: **Pacific:** Muri-Ranga-Whenua (Polynesia); **Bering:** Sedna (Inuit);

The ancient Romans believed that Neptune was god of the sea. He is often shown holding a three-pointed spear called a trident.

God of paradise

The Hawaiian Islands are in the northern central Pacific. Legend tells that the god Maui went fishing one day and hooked a great piece of seabed. As he reeled it in, it broke at the surface into eight pieces, which became a chain of beautiful islands—the Hawaiian Islands. We know now that the Hawaiian Islands are the tips of seabed volcanoes.

Fighting with sharks

On some Pacific islands, it is the custom for young men to battle with sharks. These dangerous fish are lured into a shallow lagoon with special rattles, animal meat, or blood. If the young men can catch or kill a shark, they prove their strength and manhood.

On other islands, people believe that sharks are the spirits of their ancestors, or even gods. They believe that sharks should never be harmed or caught.

The Parting of the Red Sea

The Bible tells how God instructed Moses to lead his people, the Israelites, from their exile in Egypt to the Promised Land. Moses led them toward the Red Sea, which seemed like an uncrossable barrier. Suddenly the waters parted, and they could walk across in safety. But as Egyptian soldiers pursued them, the waters surged back and the soldiers drowned.

Moses and his people were safe as the Red Sea flooded back.

Mediterranean: Poseidon (ancient Greece); **Atlantic:** Atlantis—island of ancient legend.

Exploring and Discovering

The first explorers had few maps and little idea of how the Earth was shaped. Many thought the world was flat. But through the centuries, sailors ventured out across unknown seas and oceans and discovered new lands with which to trade or conquer.

A dhow—a traditional seagoing boat of Arab regions in the Middle East and Africa.

Mapping the world

From the 1400s, technology had made it possible for skilled sailors to navigate to the far corners of the world. They drew charts (maps), opened up new trade routes, and some shared in fabulous riches.

• **1492** Christopher Columbus crossed the Atlantic and reached the "New World" of the Americas.

In 1728 Vitus Bering explored and gave his name to the Bering Sea. In 1741 he died on the island that now also bears his name.

• **1497–98** Vasco da Gama sailed around the southern tip of Africa and reached India.

• **1519–21** Ferdinand Magellan led the first round-the-world voyage, passing the tip of South America into the Pacific.

• **1768–71** James Cook explored the South Pacific and charted the coasts of New Zealand and eastern Australia.

The world map of land, sea, and ocean was becoming complete.

Early explorers: **Mediterranean:** Minoans of Crete 2000 B.C.; **Atlantic:** (South) Dias 1488;

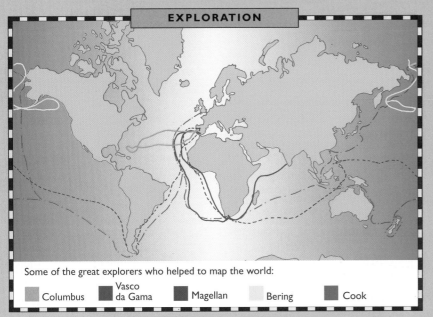

EXPLORATION

Some of the great explorers who helped to map the world:

- Columbus
- Vasco da Gama
- Magellan
- Bering
- Cook

The early explorers charted the seas and oceans to discover new lands and new trade routes.

Seagoing Warriors

The Baltic Sea in northern Europe was home to the Vikings, great sailors and warriors. They navigated across the open seas in their strong longships that were built to survive in rough conditions. They sailed into the North Sea and then across the Atlantic in search of new lands in which to settle.

Longships carried Vikings across the Atlantic to North America.

Shortcuts

The modern sea route between Europe and the Far East is along the Suez Canal, in northeast Egypt. It links the Mediterranean with the Red Sea and Indian Ocean. It is 105 miles (169km) long and cuts more than 6,250 miles (10,000km) off the route around Africa.

Another vital shortcut is the 51-mile (82-km) Panama Canal, in Central America. It links the Pacific and Atlantic oceans, saving a trip of more than 6,830 miles (11,000km) around South America.

The Corinth Canal shortens the distance between the Adriatic Sea and Athens by over 200 miles (320km). Its width plus strong currents make it hard to navigate.

Caribbean: Columbus 1492; **Pacific:** de Balboa 1513; **Bering:** Bering 1720s to 1741.

Living off the Sea

The oceans were once teeming with fish and shellfish; it seemed that the "harvest of the seas" would never end. But today's fishing fleets find it more difficult to locate large shoals. Overfishing and increasingly polluted seas are seriously reducing our fish stocks.

Traditional nets and poles catch only small numbers of fish.

Traditional methods

Coastal peoples have always harvested shellfish by hand, used small nets for shoals of little fish and prawns, and speared larger sea creatures. Inuit people hunt seals and walruses along the cold shores of the Bering Sea. Pacific islanders trapped swordfish and marlin. These traditional methods did little to reduce the numbers of marine animals or upset the balance of nature.

Even with modern equipment catching large fish like tuna can be difficult and dangerous.

More and bigger catches

But the balance began to shift as Atlantic fishing boats became larger and faster. No part of the sea was out of reach. Large-scale hunting of fish, squid, krill, whales, seals, and other marine life began to reduce the numbers of these animals, which could not breed fast enough to keep up.

Important fish: **Pacific:** sardines and anchovies; **Atlantic:** cod and herring;

High-tech fishing

Today, fishing is a science. Fast ocean trawlers locate shoals using echo sounders and scoop them up in vast nets. The fish are cleaned, processed, and frozen within hours, ready for the supermarket shelves. The main Atlantic fisheries are over shallow continental shelf areas, where haddock, hake, mackerel, flounder, eel, and lobster are caught.

All fished out?

Fish numbers are falling yearly. Too many immature fish are caught, so reducing the numbers that will be able to breed and increase the fish stock. Fishing laws have been changed to save the remaining stocks. But sadly, the main result seems to be disputes between nations and among fishing crews about who can catch what's left.

The Arctic Ocean is the smallest ocean but contains the richest fishing grounds. Warm currents flow north from the Pacific and Atlantic, and mix with the icy polar waters, bringing up nutrients from the shallow seabed. More nutrients pour in from the rivers of northern Asia, North America, and northern Europe. In summer, the sun shines continually for almost six months. These conditions allow plankton to thrive, and they support all kinds of fish, whales, seals, and seabirds.

Laws govern the areas that can be fished, the types, size, and weight of fish caught, and the size of the holes in the nets. But the laws are often broken.

In Arctic seas, the Inuit people catch fish through holes cut in the ice.

Mediterranean: monkfish; **Caribbean:** red snapper; **Bering:** halibut.

Fun by the Sea

The seaside is great fun for vacations. Around many oceans and seas, tourism is the biggest industry. This is especially true of the Caribbean Sea, where the local island people earn most of their living from the leisure industry. The Bahamas, Jamaica, the Cayman and Virgin Islands, Grenada, and Trinidad and Tobago are seen as tropical vacation paradises.

Massive ocean liners carry passengers on luxury cruises to exotic places.

Soaking up the sun

At many tropical island destinations, the tourists who come to wonder at the beauty can also help to ruin the environment they have come to enjoy. Large numbers of tourists need food, drink, and places to stay. This puts a strain on the islands' limited garbage disposal, fresh water supplies, and sewage systems.

Some souvenirs and trinkets are made from sea creatures or their parts, such as branches of coral and conch shells. This may bring money into the region, but it also helps to destroy the wildlife.

If global warming melts polar ice caps and raises sea levels, islands such as the Maldives in the Indian Ocean could disappear below the waves!

Water sports

Seaside activity vacations involving water sports are a boom business. People can swim, sail, surf, windsurf, water-ski, jet-ski, and fly in seaplanes and balloons. They can go seaangling, frolic with dolphins, take a pedal boat around the bay, or gaze

Surfers challenge wind and waves.

through a glass-bottomed boat at the wildlife below. They can snorkel or scuba dive among the hundreds of coral reefs that fringe tropical islands and coasts.

The biggest Reef

The Great Barrier Reef, in the Coral Sea off northeast Australia, is the largest and most spectacular collection of coral reefs in the world. It is about 1,400 miles (2,000km) long and covers an area larger than the size of Florida, U.S. Tourists can stay in basic campsites, or in floating luxury hotels directly over the coral! The authorities are eager to prevent exploitation and damage, and many marine nature reserves are dotted along the reef's length.

Branching corals near the Barrier Reef's Heron Island.

Threats

But again, tourism can bring problems. Boat keels and propellers damage the coral and frighten sea animals. Oil and fuel leak into the water. Fortunately, some governments recognize the need to preserve these habitats. The Caribbean, for example, now has over fifty marine parks and nature reserves, and more are planned. Eco-tourism allows people to visit an area and enjoy the wildlife while causing the least disturbance.

Mediterranean: Majorca; **Caribbean:** Jamaica; **Bering:** not a tourist destination.

Ocean Riches

Like sailors in olden days, modern explorers also search the seas for riches. They look for oil and gas, or rocks rich in minerals and metals. Waves and tides could provide clean, renewable energy sources. And marine plants and animals might yield new drugs for medicines.

Global trade

The oceans also provide important modern trade routes. Giant cargo ships carry goods around the world. Their loads vary from cars and washing machines, to frozen meat and preserved fruits, to clothes and shoes.

Huge cranes unload oceangoing cargo ships.

Fuels from the seabed

Oil and gas are vital to today's world, for fuels such as gasoline, and for materials like plastics. They formed from the fossilized remains of plants and animals that lived millions of years ago and are now trapped in rocks deep under the seabed. Holes are drilled into the ocean floor. If they strike lucky, a production platform is placed over the site to pump oil or gas to the surface, along a pipeline or into a supertanker

An offshore oil platform burns waste gases.

Overexploited resources: **Pacific:** pearls, conch shells; **Atlantic:** whalebone, walrus ivory

Metals and gems

Some of the sea's natural resources are very rare. In certain areas, the ocean bed is littered with lumps or nodules of rock that are rich in rare metals such as manganese. These can be trawled up with huge nets on very long towlines and used in industry.

Even rarer, and much more beautiful, are the glistening pearls found in oysters. These are now farmed along some coasts. The oysters grow on wooden poles or fences put in shallow water. A tiny piece of irritating grit is placed inside each shell. The creature protects itself by covering this with layers of smooth, pale mineral—the pearl.

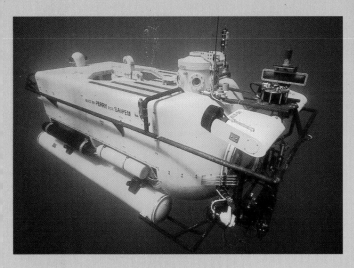

Deep-sea submersibles have very thick metal hulls to withstand the enormous pressures found in the depths.

Uncharted territory

The ocean depths are the last great unexplored regions on earth. They are freezing cold and pitch black, as the sun's rays cannot filter beyond the shallow surface waters. And the weight of the thousands of feet of water above produces huge pressures. A tiny fraction of the ocean depths has been explored in deep-sea submersibles that are built to withstand the extreme conditions, but there are regions of the deep sea that no one has ever seen.

Oil to Water

The Middle East is a hot, dry region, with limited natural fresh water for its people. But almost all around is salt water—the Red and Arabian seas, the Mediterranean Sea, and the Persian Gulf. Seawater can be turned into fresh water by removing the salt, a process called desalination. This needs large amounts of energy and machinery, which makes it very expensive. The Middle East has the wealth of its oil fields, so it can afford this process.

Desalination plants turn salt water into drinking water.

Mediterranean: sponges; **Caribbean:** giant clams; **Bering:** fur seals.

Keeping the Oceans Clean

For thousands of years people have used the oceans as the "world's trash can," out of sight, below the waves, it was hoped all kinds of garbage and wastes would decay into seabed mud. The oceans were so big, they would never become full. We now know this is wrong.

Accidents

Oceans are home to fragile communities that can be badly damaged by pollution. Some of the worst pollution occurs when supertankers spill oil into the seas. One of the worst was the *Exxon Valdez* disaster. This tanker ran aground in the North Pacific near Alaska, in 1989. Its cargo of crude oil spread over 1,850 square miles (4,800 sq km) of ocean and along 800 miles (1,300km) of coastline.

Oil-soaked seabirds find it impossible to clean themselves.

An open sewer

For thousands of years, people have used the seas as sewers. But ports, coastal cities, and vacation areas have ever more people. They all produce sewage, dirty water, and solid wastes. In some regions, untreated industrial chemicals pour straight into the sea. Some are so toxic, or poisonous, that even a minute amount kills all forms of life.

Sewage outfall pipes cross the shore and continue under the waves to release the wastes further out at sea. But tides and currents may bring waste back again.

Animals under threat: **Pacific:** white-sided dolphin; **Atlantic:** bottle-nose whale;

Mediterranean monk seals are among the world's rarest sea mammals.

Pollution danger zones

The pollution problem is greatest in seas that are relatively enclosed. The Mediterranean Sea's only natural link to a large ocean (the Atlantic) is through the narrow Strait of Gibraltar. The North Sea is shallow and similarly narrow at the English Channel. There is only a limited amount of water to carry away the wastes from people and industries around the coasts.

International effort

Preventing pollution is expensive and difficult. It needs international cooperation and new views about the "Laws of the Sea." But if we do not stop dumping industrial chemicals, sewage, rubbish, and nuclear wastes, or if we fail to control our fishing and hunting of marine life, our seas and oceans will be damaged beyond repair.

Safe in the South?

The vast so-called Southern Ocean surrounds the great frozen landmass of Antarctica. During the first half of this century its waters ran red with the blood of millions of great whales, slaughtered as they fed on the rich summer krill and plankton. Some species were hunted almost to extinction. In 1994, most of the world's nations agreed to a huge marine nature reserve, the Southern Ocean Sanctuary, where whaling and similar hunting is completely banned.

Garbage on the beach is just one of the threats facing the earth's seas and oceans.

Mediterranean: monk seal: **Caribbean:** Caribbean manatee; **Bering:** Steller's sea lion.

Glossary

bar In the context of seas, this is sand and gravel carried along the coast by longshore drift and deposited to form a bank.

condense When a gas or vapor turns into a liquid.

continent A major landmass on the earth's surface.

continental shelf The relatively shallow seabed off the shores of continents.

continental slope The steep drop between the continental shelf and the deep ocean floor.

crust The earth's "skin," the relatively thin outer, solid layer of rock that floats on the hot, partly liquid layer beneath.

current Water flowing steadily in a particular direction, like the flow of a river or ocean currents.

density The mass of a given volume of a substance, usually measured as pounds per cubic foot. The density of liquids, for example, sea water, can vary with their temperature and saltiness.

dissolve When a substance, such as salt, mixes into a liquid and becomes part of that liquid.

evolution Gradual change that living things undergo over many generations, which makes them better able to survive.

fog Thick cloud of droplets of water suspended in the air near to the earth's surface, which are difficult to see through.

fossil fuels Includes coal, oil, and natural gas, which can be burned to produce energy. Formed from prehistoric plants and animals that turned to fossils over millions of years.

gravity The natural force of attraction between two very heavy bodies, such as the moon and the earth.

hydrothermal vent A crack in the seabed near a deep oceanic ridge, where hot water gushes up from below. It supports unique communities of animals.

lithosphere Layer of rocks that covers the earth's surface, made of the solid crust plus the outer, solid part of the layer below.

lithospheric plates Massive jigsaw-like slabs of rock which make up the lithosphere, and which move very slowly and carry the continents with them.

longshore drift Movement of sand and shingle along a beach as they are carried by currents and waves.

marine To do with the sea.

minerals Natural substances that make up the Earth's rocks. There are more than 3,000 types.

mist Fine droplets of water carried in the air near the ground.

nutrients Essential substances that living things need to stay alive, grow, maintain, and repair their bodies, and keep healthy.

oceanic crust Formed from molten rock welling up between lithospheric plates.

oceanic ridge An undersea mountain range formed where plates are moving apart.

plankton Microscopic animals (zooplankton) and plants (phytoplankton) that drift through the surface waters of the oceans. They provide food for many larger animals.

renewable Replaceable without using up the earth's resources.

salt Sodium chloride, also known as rock salt, sea salt, and table salt. It dissolves easily in water. As seawater dries, or evaporates, it leaves salt deposits.

spit Sand and gravel carried along the coast by longshore drift and deposited to form a hooked ridge, joined to the shore at one end.

subduction Where two lithospheric plates meet and one is pushed down beneath the other.

tide The regular up-and-down movement of the surface of seas and oceans, mainly caused by the pull or gravity of the moon.

tropical In the belt of land and sea around the earth's middle, to either side of the equator, where the climate is mostly hot and damp.

water vapor Invisible type of gas formed when water gets warm and evaporates.

Fact File

The Oceans: areas in millions of square miles (sq km)

NAME	AREA		PROPORTION OF TOTAL OCEAN AREA	GREATEST DEPTH (in feet)	(in meters)	AVERAGE DEPTH (in feet)	(in meters)
Pacific	69	(180)	50%	35,799	10,911	14,108	4,300
Atlantic	36	(94)	26%	28,374	8,648	12,140	3,700
Indian	28	(74)	21%	25,346	7,725	12,796	3,900
Arctic	5	(12)	3%	16,805	5,122	4,364	1,330

Seas, Bays, and Gulfs

NAME	AREA million sq miles	million sq km
Coral	1.8	4.7
Arabian	1.5	3.8
South China	1.4	3.6
Mediterranean	1.1	3.0
Caribbean	1.0	2.5
Bering	0.9	2.3
Bay of Bengal	0.8	2.1
Sea of Okhotsk	0.6	1.6
Gulf of Mexico	0.5	1.5
Gulf of Guinea	0.5	1.5

In contrast, all five of the Great Lakes in North America have an area of only 0.09 million square miles (0.25 million sq km).

Smallest Sea
One of the smallest named seas is also the coldest: It is the White Sea, off the Arctic Ocean, at 0.03 million square miles (0.09 million sq km).

Highest Seamount
The highest seamount (underwater mountain) is between Samoa and New Zealand and rises 28,545 feet (8,700m) from its base near the Tonga Trench.

Sea Temperatures
The water temperature at the surface of the sea varies between 28°F (–2°C) in the Arctic Ocean to 97°F (36°C) in the Persian Gulf. The highest temperatures anywhere in the oceans are at hydrothermal vents (or black smokers) where the water spurts out at over 752°F (400°C).

Biggest Tsunami
The highest tsunami, or "tidal wave," (which has nothing to do with tides but is caused by an undersea earthquake) reached 1,719 feet (524m) in height along the shore of Alaska, in 1958.

Clearest Sea
The clearest seawater is in the Weddell Sea, off Antarctica, with visibility reaching 262 feet (80m) in good conditions. In parts of the North Sea, visibility is less than 3 feet (1m).

Biggest Current
The biggest and fastest ocean current is the Antarctic Circumpolar Current, which flows at a rate of 185 million tons (168 million tonnes) of water per second.

Biggest Icebergs
Huge chunks of ice sometimes break away from the ice shelves that jut out across the sea around Antarctica. The largest ever seen was about 210 miles (335km) long and 61 miles (97km) wide. The highest icebergs have been recorded in the Northern Hemisphere. One seen off Greenland in 1959 was 341 feet (167m) high.

A flock of birds above the icy waters of the Antarctic.

Index